QUESTIONS EXPLORED

WHAT ARE THE RISKS OF VAPING?

by Bev Crawford

BrightPoint Press

San Diego, CA

© 2023 BrightPoint Press
an imprint of ReferencePoint Press, Inc.
Printed in the United States

For more information, contact:
BrightPoint Press
PO Box 27779
San Diego, CA 92198
www.BrightPointPress.com

ALL RIGHTS RESERVED.

No part of this work covered by the copyright hereon may be reproduced or used in any form or by any means—graphic, electronic, or mechanical, including photocopying, recording, taping, web distribution, or information storage retrieval systems—without the written permission of the publisher.

Content Consultant: Michael Blaha, M.D., M.P.H., Ciccarone Center for the Prevention of Cardiovascular Disease, Johns Hopkins University

---

LIBRARY OF CONGRESS CATALOGING-IN-PUBLICATION DATA

Names: Crawford, Bev, author.
Title: What are the risks of vaping? / by Bev Crawford.
Description: San Diego, CA: BrightPoint Press, [2023] | Series: Questions explored | Includes bibliographical references and index. | Audience: Grades 7-9
Identifiers: LCCN 2022029126 (print) | LCCN 2022029127 (eBook) | ISBN 9781678205041 (hardcover) | ISBN 9781678205058 (pdf)
Subjects: LCSH: Vaping--Juvenile literature. | Electronic cigarettes--Juvenile literature. | Teenagers--Tobacco use--Juvenile literature. | Nicotine addiction--Juvenile literature.
Classification: LCC HV5748 .C73 2023 (print) | LCC HV5748 (eBook) | DDC 362.29/60835--dc23/eng/20220811
LC record available at https://lccn.loc.gov/2022029126
LC eBook record available at https://lccn.loc.gov/2022029127

CONTENTS

AT A GLANCE   4

INTRODUCTION   6
    CHOOSING A PATH

CHAPTER ONE   12
    WHERE DID VAPING COME FROM?

CHAPTER TWO   28
    WHAT DOES VAPING DO TO THE BODY?

CHAPTER THREE   48
    WHAT DO TEENS SAY ABOUT VAPING?

CHAPTER FOUR   62
    HOW ARE PEOPLE FIGHTING
    AGAINST VAPING?

Glossary   74
Source Notes   75
For Further Research   76
Index   78
Image Credits   79
About the Author   80

AT A GLANCE

- People have been smoking tobacco for thousands of years. E-cigarettes are more recent tobacco products. They were introduced in the 2000s. Using e-cigarettes is called vaping.

- E-cigarettes contain an addictive drug called nicotine. Some e-cigarettes have more nicotine than regular cigarettes.

- Tobacco companies target kids. Almost all smokers and vapers start as young people. When young people smoke and vape, they become new customers for tobacco companies.

- Vaping is not good for the body. It can harm the lungs, heart, and brain. The effects of vaping are still being studied.

- Many young people have had health problems because of vaping. EVALI is a new lung disease caused by vaping.

- The US Food and Drug Administration (FDA) regulates tobacco products. But there are a lot of new tobacco products. The FDA's rules have not been enough to keep e-cigarettes away from kids.

- Many young people want to quit vaping. But nicotine addiction makes it hard to stop. Influencers are trying to help by talking about quitting on social media and inspiring others to quit.

- People can help each other quit vaping. They can set a good example by choosing not to vape.

INTRODUCTION

CHOOSING A PATH

Alex loved playing on her high school soccer team. She and her teammates had worked hard at their practices this year. Alex could run faster. Her passes went farther. She had even scored a few goals. Alex thought her team could win the championship.

Peer pressure is one of the most common ways teens are introduced to vaping.

One day, Alex saw some other players blowing clouds of steam. It looked cool.

"What are you doing?" she asked.

E-cigarettes are very addictive. Once a person starts vaping, it can be hard to quit.

They showed her an e-cigarette. They let her try it. At first, she coughed. But soon it felt better. It was called vaping. Vaping means inhaling from an e-cigarette.

Soon, Alex got her own e-cigarette from a friend. At first, she just vaped a little. She liked feeling a buzz. Then she started to vape every day. Soon, she felt bad if she did not vape. She needed to vape just to feel normal.

Alex's soccer coach found out that some players were vaping. Coach talked to everyone about the dangers of vaping. She said nicotine is **addictive**. Nicotine is the addictive drug in tobacco. It is bad for your lungs and heart. Vaping was against school rules.

Alex did not know her e-cigarette had so much nicotine. Since she started vaping, it had become harder to breathe. She could not run as fast. She did not want to vape anymore. But when she tried to stop, she had headaches. She had trouble sleeping. Alex realized she was having **withdrawal symptoms**. She was addicted.

Alex decided to ask the school nurse for help. Together, they made a plan to quit. Quitting was hard. But gradually, Alex's breathing got easier. Her running improved. Alex told her teammates that the nurse helped her quit. The nurse could help them too.

The first playoff game was coming up. The team would be traveling and staying at a hotel. Coach talked to the team about the trip. Vaping was not allowed. If a player got

Teens who want to quit vaping can talk to a trusted adult for help.

caught vaping, she would be sent home. She would be kicked off the team.

But that night, two players vaped in their hotel room. Coach caught them. The players were sent home. They were kicked off the team. Alex decided to tell her parents what happened. She never wanted to vape again.

CHAPTER ONE

WHERE DID VAPING COME FROM?

Scientists believe that people began smoking tobacco more than 6,000 years ago. People discovered wild tobacco in what is now South America. They bred plants to have larger leaves and more nicotine. These new plants spread north into what are now Central and North

Tobacco has been a popular product around the world since the late 1600s.

America. More people began using the stronger plants. They liked the way tobacco made them feel. It gave them a pleasant sense of energy.

European explorers arrived in the region in 1492. By then, Indigenous people were using many kinds of tobacco. Tobacco was seen as a plant with great power. It was used in rituals, ceremonies, and medicines. Indigenous people showed the Europeans how to use tobacco. Europeans thought tobacco was special. They took it back to Europe, where people began smoking.

THE HISTORY OF SMOKING

In the 1500s, tobacco was farmed in British and American colonies. By the late 1600s, tobacco had become more accepted in Europe. It grew into a global

Tobacco was a popular crop in the American colonies.

trade product. People enjoyed chewing and smoking tobacco.

By 1850, smoking was common throughout the world. Affordable, mass-produced cigarettes appeared

Throughout the 1940s and 1950s, many people smoked cigarettes regularly.

16

in 1890 and quickly became popular. Tobacco companies advertised heavily. By 1950, about half of the population of industrialized countries smoked. At the same time, scientists found evidence that linked smoking with lung **cancer**. More research showed other negative health effects of smoking. By 1978, only 33 percent of American adults smoked.

By the end of the twentieth century, everyone knew tobacco was addictive. It was one of the leading causes of disease and death around the world. American tobacco companies were sued over the costs of health care provided to smokers. In 1998, this resulted in the Master Settlement Agreement. Tobacco companies had to pay $206 billion to US states. They also had to help fund research about smoking. The money was payback for taxpayer dollars that had been spent to provide care for smoking-related illnesses. Tobacco companies were also not allowed to advertise to people under the age of eighteen. Still, health experts said in 2016 that cigarette smoking was the primary cause of premature death in the United States.

HISTORY OF E-CIGARETTES

The first electronic cigarette appeared in 1963. It was created as a way to smoke without combustion, or burning. In 2003, the modern e-cigarette was invented by

---

TRUTH INITIATIVE

The Master Settlement Agreement was created to pay states back for health care costs related to smoking. The agreement also provided funding for a new group called "Truth Initiative." The group works to prevent youth tobacco use. Truth Initiative publishes studies in academic journals. It tells the truth about nicotine. It helps teach people across the country about the dangers of tobacco. Truth Initiative has also helped millions of teens quit cigarettes and vaping.

a Chinese pharmacist. He was a smoker. He wanted another way to smoke. First, the user inhales on an e-cigarette. This causes a small battery to heat a liquid. The liquid usually contains nicotine. An e-cigarette also has an atomizer, which is a device that turns liquid into mist. The mist has very tiny particles, like a vapor. That is why it is called vaping.

Soon, the e-cigarette hit the US market. Companies said it could replace regular cigarettes. Copycat manufacturers rushed to sell their own versions. They used cool designs and marketing. This made vaping

Many e-cigarettes come in flavors that are meant to appeal to kids and teens.

more socially acceptable than smoking. Fewer people were using cigarettes. Tobacco companies were losing money in cigarette sales. So they came out with their own e-cigarette brands. Vaping was a new market for tobacco companies. And that new market had few rules.

Teen vaping has become a major problem in the United States.

THE TOBACCO INDUSTRY TARGETS KIDS

American vaping and tobacco companies quickly introduced many flavors. Some were sweet, such as "Chocolate Treat," "Cherry

Crush," and "Banana Cream Pie." Young celebrities vaped. E-cigarettes were sold in convenience stores. Suddenly, e-cigarettes were more popular among teenagers than regular cigarettes.

Tobacco companies studied the smoking habits of teens. They created products and marketing plans aimed at them. Philip Morris is one of the world's largest tobacco companies. In 2006, it said, "Today's teenager is tomorrow's potential regular customer, and the overwhelming majority of smokers first begin to smoke while still in their teens."[1] The tobacco industry says that e-cigarettes are less harmful than regular cigarettes. They use this claim to justify marketing their products to kids. It makes e-liquids in flavors that kids and teens like. It also uses **targeted advertising** to make teens want to buy tobacco products. When teens buy the products, the tobacco companies make money.

VAPING TODAY

Most teens start vaping with flavored e-cigarettes. The most common flavors are fruit, candy, mint, and menthol. One study showed that flavors are the main reason teens try vaping. E-cigarettes can also be

Tobacco companies use targeted advertising to attract teens to their products.

used for other drugs, such as **marijuana**.

Another study showed that teens who vape are seven times more likely to smoke cigarettes in the future.

Federal, state, and city government agencies are trying to stop teen vaping. A 2015 report studied the minimum age to buy tobacco products. It found that raising the minimum age to 21 "could

E-CIGARETTES REGULATED AS TOBACCO PRODUCTS

In 2009, the Family Smoking Prevention and Tobacco Control Act was created. Under this act, the FDA makes rules about e-cigarettes. The act controls parts of the tobacco industry. It limits tobacco marketing and sales to young people. It also requires smokeless tobacco products to have warning labels. For example, a label might say, "WARNING: This product can cause gum disease and tooth loss." The act requires companies to list ingredients on tobacco products too.

prevent 223,000 deaths among people born between 2000 and 2019."[2] In 2019, Congress passed a law that raised the minimum age to 21. In 2020, the FDA banned flavored cartridges, or e-liquid containers, except for tobacco and menthol. But e-cigarettes could still undo much of the progress made in reducing cigarette smoking. Many other flavored products, such as disposable e-cigarettes, were still legal after the FDA's ban. In 2020, the use of flavored disposable e-cigarettes went up a thousand percent among high schoolers.

CHAPTER TWO

WHAT DOES VAPING DO TO THE BODY?

Vaping is bad for the body. It hurts the lungs, the heart, and even the brain. Studies have shown that vaping is worse for teens than for adults. The teenage lungs are still growing and developing. So is the teenage brain. Vaping can change the way the teenage body develops.

A single Juul pod contains as much nicotine as twenty cigarettes.

NICOTINE

The liquid in most e-cigarettes contains nicotine. Nicotine is a drug in tobacco. It is very addictive. Using nicotine during the teen years can harm the developing brain. Studies show nicotine can affect learning, memory, and attention. It can also make someone more likely to get addicted to other drugs.

One e-cigarette brand is Juul. It makes pods, or containers, of e-liquids. All Juul pods contain nicotine. Each pod has as much nicotine as twenty cigarettes. Vaping nicotine is easier than smoking a cigarette. That means it is easier to inhale more nicotine. It is easier to get addicted to nicotine and damage the body.

Some e-cigarette brands say their products contain **synthetic** nicotine. Synthetic nicotine is created in a laboratory. It does not come from the tobacco plant.

But it is still nicotine, and all types of nicotine are harmful.

THE LUNGS

E-cigarettes contain more than just nicotine. The vapor has tiny particles that can be inhaled deep into the lungs. There are lots

CHEMICALS HIDDEN IN E-CIGARETTES

There are many chemicals hidden in e-cigarettes. Propylene glycol can make lung cells become inflamed and die. **Formaldehyde** and benzene cause cancer. Acrolein is a weed killer. E-cigarette vapor also contains metals that can be toxic, such as zinc, cobalt, silver, and lead. Toxic metals cause many different illnesses. For example, lead can make the brain, lungs, and heart stop working the way they should.

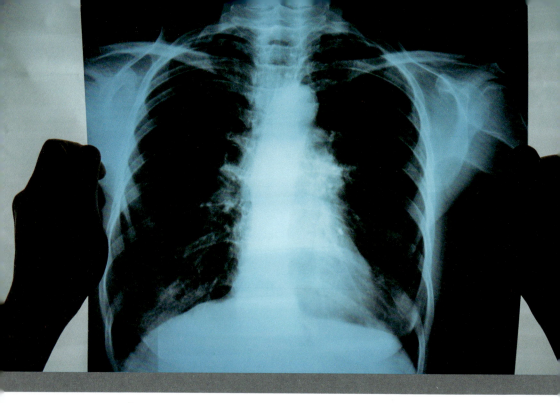

Vaping can cause serious damage to the lungs.

of chemicals in the vapor. Every flavor has a different mix of chemicals. The vapor also contains heavy metals that are poisonous.

The lungs work hard. They have two important jobs to do. The first is to take in oxygen. The lungs give the oxygen to the blood. Cells need oxygen in order to work.

The second job of the lungs is to get rid of carbon dioxide from the blood. Carbon dioxide is the waste product from cells. Too much carbon dioxide can be toxic to the body.

    The insides of the lungs look a bit like an upside-down tree. Air enters through the trachea, or the main breathing tube. The trachea branches off into the left and right lungs. It continues to branch off within each lung. At the end of the branches are tiny air sacs. These are called **alveoli**. The alveoli exchange oxygen and carbon dioxide in the blood. It takes the lungs less than a minute to process all the blood in the body.

When someone vapes, the air going into her lungs is dirty. Inside the airways are cilia. These are tiny hairlike structures that work to keep the lungs clean. The cilia move together in waves. The waves move mucus, germs, and particles up toward the mouth. Then the mucus, germs, and particles can be coughed or sneezed out of the body. Vaping damages the cilia so they cannot clean the air. The lungs get dirty.

Air can also carry tiny particles from air pollution or smoke. It might contain bacteria or viruses. These can make people sick. The air sacs in the lungs have their own immune cells. These special cells clean the air. But they cannot get rid of everything.

DISEASES RELATED TO VAPING

Long-term nicotine exposure can lead to airway diseases. One common disease is asthma. The airways become swollen and have too much mucus. Other diseases are bronchitis and emphysema. Bronchitis causes inflamed airways and painful coughing. Emphysema destroys the alveoli. Vaping also causes popcorn lung. Popcorn lung happens when the airways are filled with scar tissue. Popcorn factory workers got "popcorn lung" from breathing diacetyl. Diacetyl is used in most sweet-flavored vapes.

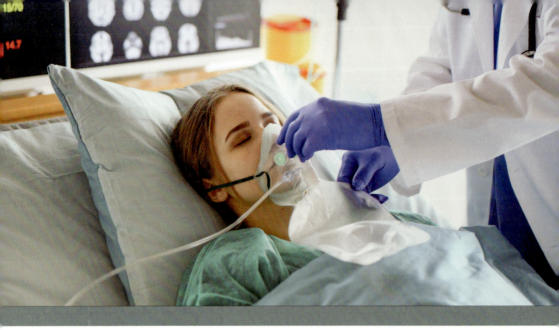

Most people with EVALI have trouble breathing and need to be hospitalized.

Vaping can overload the special cells. Sometimes the air sacs can be destroyed.

In 2019, doctors began studying a new lung disease called E-cigarette or Vaping Use-Associated Lung Injury, or EVALI. Doctors are still learning about EVALI. Most patients with EVALI have to be hospitalized. Some cannot breathe on their own.

They have to be put on a ventilator. Others have died. Doctors think one cause of EVALI is vitamin E acetate. This is added as a thickener in e-liquids containing **THC**. THC is a substance found in marijuana.

THE HEART

The heart pumps blood to the lungs and the rest of the body. Blood carries oxygen from the lungs to the muscles and the brain. The heart and lungs work together to feed the body.

E-cigarette vapor puts stress on the heart, lungs, and brain. After only a few days of vaping, the body can be damaged.

The chemical acrolein damages the lining of the heart and blood vessels. This lining is important. It keeps the heart and blood vessels healthy. When the lining is damaged, the vessels cannot fully expand. This can lead to heart attack and stroke. A heart attack happens when blood flow to the heart is blocked. A stroke happens when blood flow to the brain is stopped or reduced. Healthy blood vessels keep the heart and brain strong.

THE BRAIN

When a person vapes, nicotine reaches his brain within about ten seconds.

Nicotine from e-cigarettes can change the way the teenage brain develops.

The nicotine attaches to receptors in the brain. The brain tries to catch up. It quickly grows new nicotine receptors. This is how the brain becomes addicted to nicotine. Using nicotine during the teen years can permanently change the brain.

Compared to adults, younger people are at a greater risk of becoming addicted to substances such as nicotine.

Nicotine can affect learning, focus, and memory. It can also cause problems with impulse control and mood.

The brain keeps developing until about age twenty-five. When a teen learns a new skill, strong connections are made between brain cells. These connections are called synapses. Young brains build synapses faster than adult brains. This means young people learn faster. They make memories faster. Addiction is a form of learning. The brain learns to need nicotine.

Nicotine also affects mental health. Many people believe nicotine is relaxing. But research shows that this is not true. Nicotine can make a vaping teen feel more depressed or anxious. Nicotine does not relieve stress. It only relieves withdrawal symptoms. Quitting vaping can lead to a better mood and quality of life.

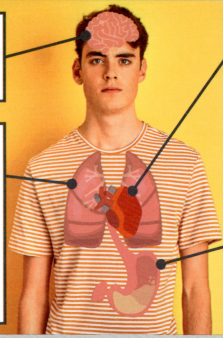

VAPING AND THE HUMAN BODY

The Brain: Nicotine rewires the young brain, causing problems with learning, focus, memory, and mood.

The Heart: Acrolein damages the lining of the heart and blood vessels. This can lead to heart attack and stroke.

The Lungs: Nicotine, acrolein, diacetyl, and other chemicals damage the lungs and cause disease. Tiny particles damage the alveoli, or air sacs, in the lungs. This means the body gets less oxygen. Blood does not get cleaned. People can get sick more easily.

The Stomach: Nicotine can cause acid reflux. This causes burning pain in the chest and makes it hard to swallow.

Source: "Health Effects," Stanford Medicine, n.d. https://med.stanford.edu/visit.html.

Vaping can have harmful effects on the human body.

THE STOMACH AND ESOPHAGUS

The esophagus is the tube that connects the throat to the stomach. It carries food and liquid from the mouth to the stomach. Nicotine can cause the muscles at the bottom of the esophagus to relax. This lets acid into the esophagus. Nicotine also causes the stomach to make more acid. This can cause acid reflux. Acid reflux happens when stomach acid rises into the esophagus. This causes painful heartburn, nausea, and bloating. Over time, acid reflux can damage the esophagus.

Nicotine also reduces the amount of saliva, the liquid in the mouth. Saliva helps with digestion. It wets food. It washes away bacteria and cleans the teeth after eating. With less saliva, it is harder for the stomach

Vaping can cause stomach problems such as heartburn and acid reflux.

to digest food. Nicotine also reduces blood flow and mucus in the esophagus. All of these effects can damage the lining of the esophagus.

Using tobacco products can make someone more likely to have esophageal cancer. The most common type of this cancer is called squamous cell carcinoma. It happens in the lining of the esophagus. It is one of the deadliest types of cancer.

WHAT HAPPENS TO THE BODY AFTER QUITTING VAPING?

When people quit vaping, they get healthier. The heartbeat and blood pressure go back to normal about twenty minutes after vaping. After a day, the risk of heart attack decreases. Oxygen levels in the blood go up. The blood vessels go back to normal. Blood circulation gets better.

Nicotine withdrawal symptoms last for about three days. "Nicotine leaves your body on day three, which is why withdrawal symptoms peak then," says Dr. Nikola Djordjevic.[3] Withdrawal symptoms include headaches, sweating, cramping, and cravings for more nicotine. The symptoms slowly go away over the next few weeks.

The lungs also get healthier. This makes it easier to breathe and smell. After a month without vaping, "your lung capacity improves," Djordjevic says.[4] There is less coughing. The lungs' immune systems get healthier too. Nine months after quitting vaping, the cilia in the airways come back. Even ten years after quitting, the body is still

Withdrawal symptoms can include cravings, depression, and trouble sleeping.

getting healthier. One study showed that ten years after quitting tobacco products, lung cancer risk is reduced by 50 percent.

Acid reflux symptoms go away after quitting too. This means that the stomach and the esophagus go back to being healthy. The pain goes away and the risk of cancer decreases.

CHAPTER THREE

WHAT DO TEENS SAY ABOUT VAPING?

Today, teens and young adults know a lot about vaping. Some still choose to vape. But many are trying to help others learn to quit. High school senior Cole Kosch made a documentary about vaping. It was for his Eagle Scout project in Austin, Texas. Another high school senior named Yuan

Some teens have started using disposable e-cigarettes.

Uy joined Raze in West Virginia. Raze is a nonprofit organization led by kids ages eleven to eighteen. Their mission is to change the culture of tobacco use. They share the truth about vaping and tobacco.

WHY TEENS VAPE

Juul brand e-cigarettes are popular. They are small and easy to hide. They often look like a sleek high-tech gadget or flash drive. Juul pods use a special kind of nicotine called nicotine salts. The salts are less irritating to the throat. They make it easier to inhale high levels of nicotine.

Many young people started vaping because of the sweet flavors. Then the FDA banned most e-cigarette flavors. Now Juul pods have only two flavors: tobacco and menthol. Many kids started using the menthol flavor. Some use flavored disposable e-cigarettes, such as Puff Bars. These come in all sorts of sweet flavors such as Strawberry, Mango, and

Many teens who vape are worried about their health.

Lemon Ice. Disposables are much cheaper than Juul. Some have even more nicotine. Others have synthetic nicotine. Puff Bar products also use bright colors and cool names. These make teens want to buy the product. In fact, 97 percent of vapers ages fifteen to twenty-one use flavored e-cigarettes.

WHY TEENS QUIT

Many young people want to quit vaping. They want to be free from addiction. They do not want to spend their money on e-cigarettes. They are also worried about their health. A 2020 survey asked young people why they want to quit vaping.

The most common answer was health concerns. Many people who took the survey said their lungs were weak. They had trouble breathing. Another survey found that most young people believe that tobacco and vaping companies lie about the safety of vaping.

Teens can use online resources to learn how to quit vaping.

Truth Initiative started a campaign called Quit Together. Influencers publicly announced their intention to quit vaping on TikTok. Then they documented their quitting process on TikTok, inviting their followers to quit too. They used an app called This Is Quitting. The app is free and anonymous. Users get one age-appropriate message each day. Before quitting, messages help them become more confident. After quitting, messages provide support for at least eight weeks. Users can use keywords to get instant support. One young adult

> **I QUIT, SO CAN YOU**
>
> "If you are vaping today, believe me when I say you are stronger than this. You can quit," says Ally Harrison. She won a scholarship from Truth Initiative in 2019. Piper Johnson is another quitter. She says, "For those who want to quit, I know how hard it is. . . . That 'nic-buzz' is not worth your life. For me, it was a really scary feeling to almost die from it—vaping is not worth it."
>
> *Quoted in "Young Ex-Vapers Share Their Experience and Advice on Quitting Vaping," Truth Initiative, March 13, 2020. https://truthinitiative.org.*

named Scarlett tried the app. She started going to the gym and working out instead of vaping.

YOUNG PEOPLE IN THE NEWS

Daniel Ament was sixteen years old. He was an athlete at Grosse Pointe North High School in Michigan. He swam and ran track. He started vaping in December 2018. Ten months later, he had trouble breathing. He had to go to the hospital. The doctors thought Daniel might have pneumonia. But he got worse very quickly. His lungs filled with fluid and dead tissue. He had to be

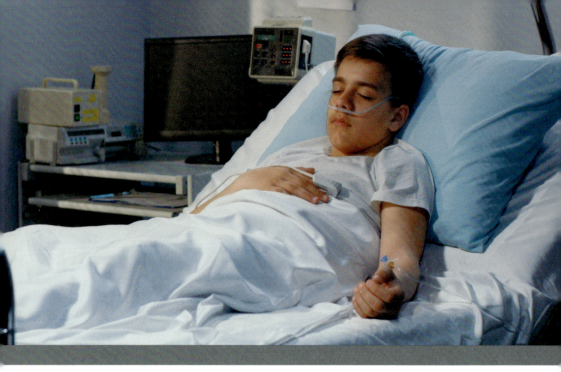

Some teens who vape can end up with serious health problems.

hooked up to a machine to stay alive. He could not breathe by himself.

The doctors told Daniel's mother that he would not live without a lung transplant. His own lungs were too damaged by EVALI. Doctor Lisa Allenspach said, "It was his only hope."[5] Daniel was placed on the Organ

Transplant Waiting List. In 2019, he had a double lung transplant. He will need to take antirejection medication for the rest of his life. This will make sure that his body does not reject the new lungs.

A seventeen-year-old in Georgia had a similar experience. He felt like he was having a heart attack. His mom took him to the emergency room. The doctor said his left lung had collapsed. The teen admitted to his mom that he had been vaping for more than a year.

Then his right lung collapsed. The doctors put a breathing tube into his chest. His lungs were covered in blisters. The blisters had popped. Air leaked into the ribcage. The air had put pressure on the lung and caused it to collapse.

HOW TEENS CAN HELP EACH OTHER

There are many ways teens can help each other and spread the word about vaping. Daniel Ament started a group called Fight4Wellness. It helps educate others about the dangers of vaping. He travels to speak to teens across the country. Teens can also use online resources. For example, Raze has a list of activities on their website. These can help teens learn more about the risks of vaping. Another option is joining an anti-vaping group, such as the #ThisIsQuitting challenge.

Some US states have banned flavored tobacco products. Many states have also set rules about where people are allowed to vape.

The doctors wanted to protect him from future lung collapse. They stapled the tops of his lungs to his ribcage. He is constantly in pain because of these staples. He says the staples are a painful reminder of how dangerous vaping can be.

Oral nicotine products such as lozenges and pouches have become popular.

THE FUTURE OF VAPING

Many anti-smoking and anti-vaping groups want the FDA to ban all flavored tobacco products. They think a ban will help protect young people from nicotine. Until then, tobacco and vaping companies will keep targeting kids.

The FDA has restricted many vaping products. But new nicotine products have been created. They are not restricted by the FDA. For example, many teens have started using oral nicotine products. Lozenges can be dissolved in the mouth like candy. Nicotine pouches fit between the lips and gums. They come in flavors such as mint, berry, and cinnamon. The brand Lucy makes lozenges and nicotine gum that it says are flavored "to mask the harshness of nicotine."[6] All of these products contain high amounts of nicotine. And all forms of nicotine have the same health dangers.

CHAPTER FOUR

HOW ARE PEOPLE FIGHTING AGAINST VAPING?

Many young people have joined the fight against teen vaping and nicotine use. They have formed groups to help educate people about vaping. Young people like Daniel Ament have even created

Many teens are sharing their stories and speaking out against teen vaping.

their own groups. The government can also play a role. Congress can pass laws about vaping. The FDA can make new rules for the tobacco industry.

WHAT SCIENTISTS SAY ABOUT TEEN VAPING

Scientists and doctors agree that teen tobacco use can damage the body. Studies show that vaping is harmful in many ways.

But vaping is still new. It will be a long time before people know its long-term effects. Dr. Frances Leslie is a professor who studies addiction and the brain. She says that a whole generation of teenagers are basically test subjects for the effects of nicotine in the brain.

Neuroscientist Dr. Marina Picciotto has studied the effects of nicotine on young mice. Her study showed that nicotine caused changes in the mice's brain cells. The mice were more sensitive to stress. But Picciotto also points out that vape liquids contain much more than nicotine. Vape liquids are not labeled with a list of

> **RESOURCES TO HELP QUIT VAPING**
>
> **SmokefreeTXT for Teens** is an app. It sends support messages to teens ages thirteen to seventeen. The **quitSTART App** is another app that helps users create their own Quit Kit. They can keep track of their progress using the kit. **Teen.smokefree.gov** can help teens who want to quit vaping. The website also offers live support and a guide called Build My Vaping Quit Plan.

Researchers are still discovering new things about the effects of vaping on teens.

ingredients. "We have labeling of all the food that we get in the supermarket," Picciotto says. "Why would we not demand that we have labeling of every [ingredient] in the vape liquid?"[7]

Psychiatrist Dr. Nora Volkow uses brain imaging to find out how drugs affect the brain. Her work shows that drug addiction is a brain disorder. "The rapid rise of teen nicotine vaping in recent years has been unprecedented and deeply concerning," she says, "since we know that nicotine is highly addictive and can be delivered at high doses by vaping devices, which may also contain other toxic chemicals that may be harmful when inhaled."[8]

LAWS RESTRICTING VAPING

The federal government relies on the FDA to regulate tobacco products. The FDA creates

The FDA makes rules about tobacco products, such as requiring them to have warning labels.

rules for the tobacco industry. Dr. Robert Califf became the FDA Commissioner in 2022. He thinks there should be strict rules about tobacco. He wants to educate everyone about the dangers of tobacco.

He supports a limit on how much nicotine can be in cigarettes.

The FDA could ban menthol-flavored tobacco products. It can make rules about synthetic nicotine. But many state and local governments grew tired of waiting. They made their own laws. Massachusetts,

> **THE FDA AND VAPING**
>
> The FDA decides if products are good for public health. The FDA was given the power to regulate tobacco products in 2009. In 2016, it began making rules about e-cigarettes. It started regulating synthetic nicotine in 2022. But at that time, millions of tobacco products were already being used by teens.

New York, and Rhode Island have banned flavored e-cigarettes. The city of Chicago also banned flavored e-cigarettes. Many cities across the country have made similar bans. In June 2022, the FDA banned Juul products. It ordered them to be removed from the US market. However, the FDA later issued a temporary stay on the ban while further review was completed.

INFLUENCERS

Nick Uhas, Tisha Alyn, and Sam Grubbs are TikTok influencers. They tried to quit vaping on social media. They partnered with Truth Initiative. The "Ready to Quit JUUL"

Social media influencers can help inspire teens to quit vaping.

Quitting vaping can lead to a happier, healthier life.

campaign shared videos of young people getting rid of their Juuls. They started a challenge on TikTok. The challenge has TikTok users throw away their Juuls in creative ways. The first challenge was called "Ice Water Trick Shot." Users threw their

Juuls into cups of ice water in fun ways. Then the users quit vaping.

Scientists and doctors are learning more about vaping every day. They do research to discover all the ways young people are affected by vaping. Their work could help people understand more about the effects of vaping. It will help all young people live healthy lives.

GLOSSARY

addictive

describing a strong habit-forming substance or activity

alveoli

small air sacs in the lungs that exchange air with the blood

cancer

a tumor that grows and invades the body

formaldehyde

an irritating gas used as a disinfectant

marijuana

the cannabis plant, smoked or consumed as a mind-altering drug

synthetic

produced artificially, not naturally

targeted advertising

advertising aimed at a specific group of people

THC

tetrahydrocannabinol, the major psychoactive substance in marijuana

withdrawal symptoms

physical and mental symptoms that occur when a person stops taking an addictive drug

SOURCE NOTES

CHAPTER ONE: WHERE DID VAPING COME FROM?

1. Quoted in Laura Bach, "Tobacco Company Marketing to Kids," *Campaign for Tobacco-Free Kids*, November 3, 2021. www.tobaccofreekids.org.

2. Quoted in "Tobacco 21 Is the Law of the Land," *American Lung Association*, December 10, 2020. www.lung.org.

CHAPTER TWO: WHAT DOES VAPING DO TO THE BODY?

3. Quoted in Kimberly Holland, "12 Things That Happen to Your Body When You Stop Vaping," *The Healthy*, May 18, 2021. www.thehealthy.com.

4. Quoted in Holland, "12 Things That Happen to Your Body When You Stop Vaping."

CHAPTER THREE: WHAT DO TEENS SAY ABOUT VAPING?

5. Quoted in "First Double Lung Transplant Patient Injured by Vaping Shares Story," *Henry Ford Health*, January 30, 2020. www.henryford.com.

6. Quoted in "New and Emerging Products That Can Get Kids Hooked on Nicotine," *Partnership to End Addiction*, April 2021. https://drugfree.org.

CHAPTER FOUR: HOW ARE PEOPLE FIGHTING AGAINST VAPING?

7. Quoted in Sarah Allen, "Teen Vaping Is Bad," *Science*, February 16, 2020. www.science.org.

8. Quoted in "Study Finds Surge of Teen Vaping Levels Off," *National Institute of Health*, December 15, 2020. www.nih.gov.

FOR FURTHER RESEARCH

BOOKS

Kari A. Cornell, *E-Cigarettes and Their Dangers*. San Diego, CA: BrightPoint Press, 2020.

Lisa Idzikowski, *The Dangers of Vaping*. New York: PowerKids Press, 2020.

Anita Louise McCormick, *Vaping*. New York: Rosen Publishing Group, 2020.

INTERNET SOURCES

Jeya Anandakumar and Kathryn Mills, "The Adolescent Brain Is Literally Awesome," *Frontiers for Young Minds*, June 25, 2020. https://kids.frontiersin.org.

Cathy Becker and Angeline Jane Bernabe, "17-Year-Old Who Received Double Lung Transplant Due to Vaping Speaks Out," *Good Morning America*, January 31, 2020. www.goodmorningamerica.com.

Cole Kosch, *Shining a Light on Teen Vaping: An Educational Film for Teens About Vaping*, n.d. www.teenvaping.org.

WEBSITES

Campaign for Tobacco-Free Kids
www.tobaccofreekids.org

Campaign for Tobacco-Free Kids has comprehensive information about tobacco, the worldwide tobacco industry, smoking, vaping, and how individuals can help.

Smokefree Teen
https://teen.smokefree.gov

Smokefree Teen has tools, tips, articles, and information to help teens take control of their vaping, including Live Chat counselors and a quitting app.

Truth Initiative
https://truthinitiative.org

Funded by the Master Settlement Agreement, Truth Initiative provides tools for prevention and quitting as well as other ways to get involved.

INDEX

addiction, 9–10, 17, 29–30, 39, 41, 52, 64, 67
Ament, Daniel, 55–57, 58, 62

Califf, Robert, 68–69
cancer, 17, 31, 44–45, 47
cigarettes, 17–18, 19, 20–21, 23–25, 27, 30, 69

disposable e-cigarettes, 27, 50–51

E-cigarette or Vaping Use-Associated Lung Injury (EVALI), 36–37, 56
e-cigarettes, 8–9, 19–21, 23, 24–25, 26, 27, 29–31, 37, 49–51, 52, 69, 70

Family Smoking Prevention and Tobacco Control Act, 26
flavored e-cigarettes and tobacco products, 22–24, 27, 36, 50–51, 60–61, 69–70

health effects of vaping, 28–47, 55–59
 brain, 28, 29, 31, 37–41, 42, 64, 67
 esophagus, 42–45, 47
 heart, 28, 31, 37–38, 42
 lungs, 28, 31–35, 37, 42, 46, 55–59
 stomach, 42–44, 47

Juul, 30, 49–51, 70, 72–73

Leslie, Frances, 64

Master Settlement Agreement, 18, 19

nicotine, 9, 12, 19, 20, 29–31, 36, 38–41, 42, 43–44, 45–46, 50–51, 60–61, 62, 64–65, 67, 69

Philip Morris, 23
Picciotto, Marina, 65–66
Puff Bars, 50–51

Quit Together, 53–55, 58
quitting vaping, 41, 45–47, 48, 52–55, 65, 70–73

Raze, 49, 58
Ready to Quit Juul, 70–73

synthetic nicotine, 30–31, 51, 69

targeted advertising, 23–24
tobacco, 9, 12–15, 17, 19, 24, 26, 29, 44, 47, 60, 64, 67–69
Truth Initiative, 19, 53–54, 70

US Food and Drug Administration (FDA), 26–27, 50, 60–61, 63, 67–70

withdrawal symptoms, 10, 41, 45–46

IMAGE CREDITS

Cover: © Aleksandr Yu/
  Shutterstock Images
5: © Aleksandr Yu/
  Shutterstock Images
7: © Diego Cervo/iStockphoto
8: © Aleksandr Yu/
  Shutterstock Images
11: © Digital Skillet/iStockphoto
13: © Danm 12/Shutterstock Images
15: © Everett Collection/
  Shutterstock Images
16: © Everett Collection/
  Shutterstock Images
21: © Vershinin 89/
  Shutterstock Images
22: © Aleksandr Yu/
  Shutterstock Images
25: © Alex Liew/iStockphoto
29: © Juan Jose Napuri/iStockphoto
32: © Ketkaew Siriwat/
  Shutterstock Images
36: © Halfpoint/iStockphoto
39: © Hsyncoban/iStockphoto
40: © Dawn Gilfillan/
  Shutterstock Images
42 (teenager): © Kraken Images/
  Shutterstock Images
42 (internal organs): © Robuart/
  Shutterstock Images
44: © Noody/Shutterstock Images
47: © Monkey Business Images/
  Shutterstock Images
49: © Yarrrrr Bright/
  Shutterstock Images
51: © Twinster Photo/iStockphoto
53: © Daniel M. Ernst/
  Shutterstock Images
56: © Evgeniy Shkolenko/iStockphoto
59: © Visual Art Studio/
  Shutterstock Images
60: © Irina Piskova/iStockphoto
63: © Monkey Business Images/
  Shutterstock Images
66: © People Images/iStockphoto
68: © Kelsey Armstrong Creative/
  Shutterstock Images
71: © Silver K Black Stock/
  Shutterstock Images
72: © Raw Pixel/Shutterstock Images

ABOUT THE AUTHOR

Bev Crawford is an author who likes to write both fiction and nonfiction for kids and adults. She lost a grandfather to emphysema and a grandmother to lung cancer. She is curious about most things, loves research, and especially enjoys hiking with her dog Dugan in the woods around Connecticut.